Pebble™ Plus

Under the Sea

Crabs

by Jody Sullivan

Consulting Editor: Gail Saunders-Smith, PhD

Consultant: Debbie Nuzzolo, Education Manager
SeaWorld, San Diego, California

Capstone press

Mankato, Minnesota

Pebble Plus is published by Capstone Press,
151 Good Counsel Drive, P.O. Box 669, Mankato, Minnesota 56002.
www.capstonepress.com

1 2 3 4 5 6 10 09 08 07 06 05

Library of Congress Cataloging-in-Publication Data
Sullivan, Jody.
    Crabs / by Jody Sullivan.
    p. cm.—(Pebble plus. Under the sea)
    Summary: "Simple text and photographs present crabs, where they live, how they look,
and what they do"—Provided by publisher.
    Includes bibliographical references and index.
    ISBN 0-7368-4269-1 (hardcover)
    1. Crabs—Juvenile literature. I. Title. II. Series: Under the sea (Mankato, Minn.)
QL444.M33S94 2006
595.3'86—dc22   2004026901

Editorial Credits
Martha E. H. Rustad and Aaron Sautter, editors; Juliette Peters, set designer; Kate Opseth, book designer;
    Kelly Garvin, photo researcher; Scott Thoms, photo editor

Photo Credits
Bruce Coleman Inc./Masa Ushioda/V&W, 18–19
Corbis/Lawson Wood, cover
Marty Snyderman, 1, 5
Michael Patrick O'Neill, 17
Pete Carmichael, 14–15
Peter Arnold, Inc./Heinz Plenge, 9
Seapics.com/James D. Watt, 6–7; Ralf Kiefner, 21
Tom Stack & Associates, Inc./Dave Fleetham, 10–11; John Gerlach, 13

Note to Parents and Teachers

The Under the Sea set supports national science standards related to the diversity and unity of life. This book describes and illustrates crabs. The images support early readers in understanding the text. The repetition of words and phrases helps early readers learn new words. This book also introduces early readers to subject-specific vocabulary words, which are defined in the Glossary section. Early readers may need assistance to read some words and to use the Table of Contents, Glossary, Read More, Internet Sites, and Index sections of the book.

Table of Contents

What Are Crabs?

Crabs are sea animals
with hard shells.

Some crabs are
larger than a person.
Other crabs are
as small as a ladybug.

Body Parts

Crabs have eight legs.

They walk sideways.

Crabs have two sharp pincers.

Crabs catch small animals

with their pincers.

pincers

Crabs have hard shells.
Their shells keep them safe
from other animals.

Crabs have two eyes.

They can pull their eyes

into their shells.

eyes

What Crabs Do

Some crabs hide

from other animals.

They cover themselves

with small shells

and seaweed.

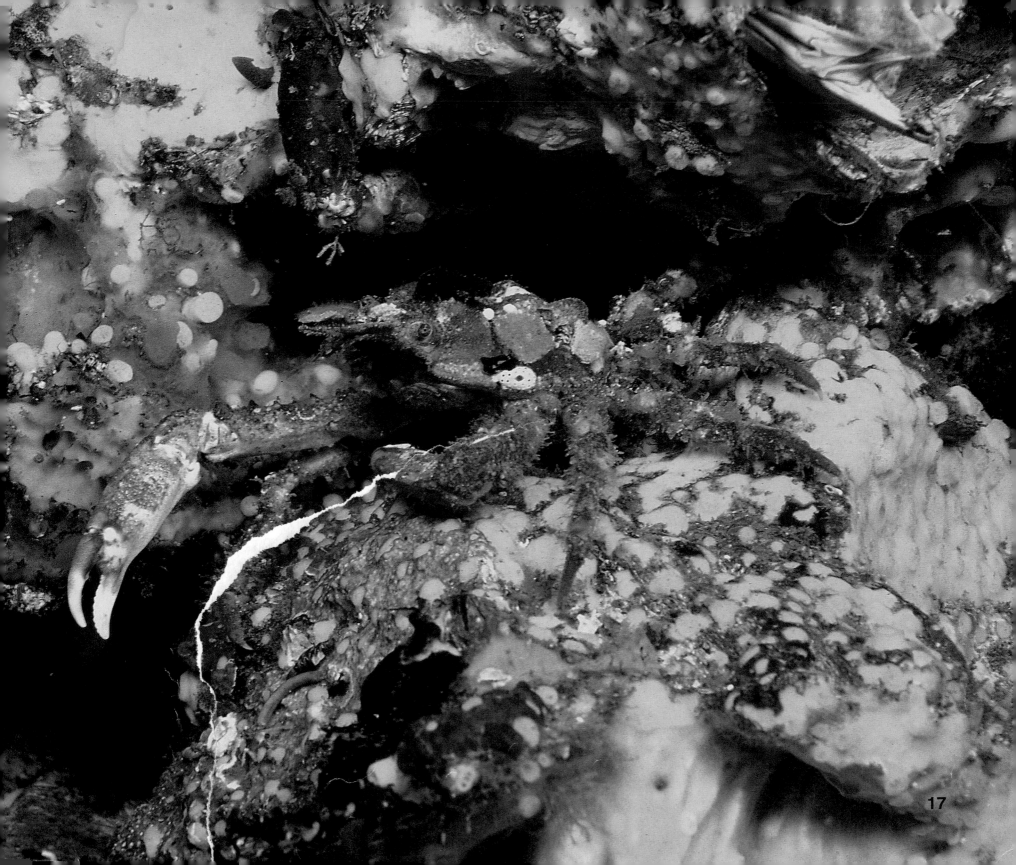

Crabs use
their pincers to fight.
Crabs fight each other
for mates.

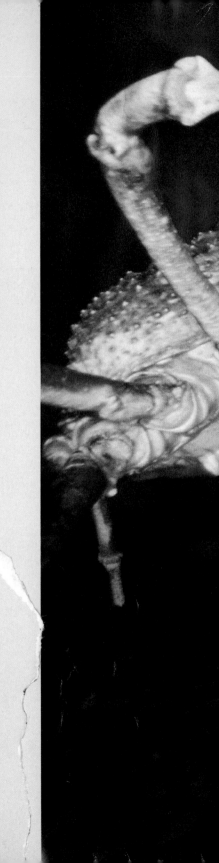

Under the Sea

Crabs live on the shore
and under the sea.

Glossary

mate—a male or female partner of a pair of animals

pincer—a pinching claw; crabs use their pincers to eat and to fight.

seaweed—a plant that grows underwater

shell—a hard outer covering; a shell protects an animal from harm.

shore—the edge of the sea, where the water meets the land; shores are covered with sand and rocks; crabs sometimes live on the shore.

sideways—from side to side

Read More

Douglas, Lloyd G. *Crab.* Ocean Life. Danbury, Conn.: Children's Press, 2005.

Hirschmann, Kris. *The Crab.* Creatures of the Sea. San Diego: Kidhaven Press, 2003.

Morgan, Sally. *Crabs and Crustaceans.* Looking at Minibeasts. North Mankato, Minn.: Thameside Press, 2001.

Internet Sites

FactHound offers a safe, fun way to find Internet sites related to this book. All of the sites on FactHound have been researched by our staff.

Here's how:

1. Visit *www.facthound.com*

2. Type in this special code **0736842691** for age-appropriate sites. Or enter a search word related to this book for a more general search.

3. Click on the **Fetch It** button.

FactHound will fetch the best sites for you!

Index

Word Count: 100
Grade: 1
Early-Intervention Level: 13